50 Outdoor Grilling Recipes for Home

By: Kelly Johnson

Table of Contents

- Classic Cheeseburgers
- Grilled Chicken Caesar Salad
- BBQ Ribs
- Grilled Corn on the Cob
- Teriyaki Salmon Skewers
- Tandoori Chicken
- Grilled Vegetable Kabobs
- Spicy Grilled Shrimp
- Garlic Butter Steak
- Hawaiian Pork Chops
- Chimichurri Grilled Lamb Chops
- Grilled Portobello Mushrooms
- Cajun Grilled Tilapia
- Honey Mustard Grilled Chicken
- Mediterranean Grilled Eggplant
- Korean BBQ Beef
- Lemon Herb Grilled Swordfish
- Chipotle Lime Grilled Corn
- Jamaican Jerk Chicken
- Maple Glazed Grilled Salmon
- Thai Peanut Grilled Tofu
- Bourbon BBQ Pork Tenderloin
- Grilled Stuffed Bell Peppers
- Garlic Rosemary Lamb Kebabs
- Chili Lime Grilled Chicken Wings
- Grilled Veggie Quesadillas
- Bacon Wrapped BBQ Shrimp
- Teriyaki Beef Skewers
- Grilled Caesar Salad
- Pineapple Rum Glazed Ham
- Moroccan Spiced Grilled Chicken
- Grilled Sausage and Peppers
- Balsamic Glazed Grilled Pork Chops
- Spicy Mango Grilled Chicken
- Grilled Halloumi Cheese

- Honey Sriracha Grilled Wings
- Grilled Ratatouille
- Argentinean Grilled Steak with Chimichurri Sauce
- Cajun Grilled Cornbread
- Grilled Stuffed Zucchini
- Lemon Garlic Grilled Shrimp
- BBQ Pulled Pork Sandwiches
- Grilled Pineapple Slices
- Buffalo Grilled Cauliflower
- Mediterranean Grilled Chicken Wraps
- Grilled Asparagus with Parmesan
- Tequila Lime Grilled Chicken
- Grilled Sweet Potato Wedges
- Ginger Soy Grilled Tofu
- BBQ Jackfruit Sandwiches

Classic Cheeseburgers

Ingredients:

- 1 pound ground beef (80/20 blend for juiciness)
- Salt and pepper, to taste
- 4 slices cheese (cheddar, American, or your preference)
- 4 hamburger buns
- Optional toppings: lettuce, tomato, onion, pickles, ketchup, mustard, mayonnaise

Instructions:

1. Preheat your grill to medium-high heat.
2. Divide the ground beef into 4 equal portions and shape each into a patty, about ¾ inch thick. Press your thumb into the center of each patty to prevent bulging while grilling. Season both sides of the patties generously with salt and pepper.
3. Place the patties on the preheated grill and cook for about 4-5 minutes on the first side, then flip and cook for an additional 3-4 minutes for medium doneness. Adjust cooking time based on your preferred level of doneness.
4. During the last minute of cooking, place a slice of cheese on each patty to melt.
5. While the patties are cooking, lightly toast the hamburger buns on the grill for about 1-2 minutes.
6. Once the cheese is melted and the patties are cooked to your liking, remove them from the grill.
7. Assemble the burgers by placing each patty on a bun and adding your desired toppings.
8. Serve immediately and enjoy the classic cheeseburgers while they're hot!

Grilled Chicken Caesar Salad

Ingredients:

- 2 boneless, skinless chicken breasts
- Salt and pepper, to taste
- 1 tablespoon olive oil
- 1 teaspoon garlic powder
- 1 teaspoon dried oregano
- 1 teaspoon dried thyme
- 1 head romaine lettuce, washed and chopped
- 1/2 cup Caesar salad dressing (homemade or store-bought)
- 1/4 cup grated Parmesan cheese
- 1 cup croutons
- Lemon wedges, for serving (optional)

Instructions:

1. Preheat your grill to medium-high heat.
2. Season the chicken breasts with salt, pepper, garlic powder, dried oregano, and dried thyme. Drizzle olive oil over the chicken and rub to coat evenly.
3. Place the seasoned chicken breasts on the preheated grill. Cook for about 6-8 minutes per side, or until the internal temperature reaches 165°F (75°C) and the chicken is cooked through. Cooking time may vary depending on the thickness of the chicken breasts.
4. Once cooked, remove the chicken from the grill and let it rest for a few minutes. Then, slice the chicken into thin strips.
5. In a large bowl, combine the chopped romaine lettuce, sliced grilled chicken, and Caesar salad dressing. Toss until the lettuce is evenly coated with the dressing.
6. Add grated Parmesan cheese and croutons to the salad bowl. Toss again to combine all the ingredients.
7. Divide the salad among serving plates or bowls.
8. Serve the grilled chicken Caesar salad immediately, garnished with additional Parmesan cheese and croutons if desired. Optionally, serve with lemon wedges on the side for squeezing over the salad before eating. Enjoy your delicious and satisfying meal!

BBQ Ribs

Ingredients:

- 2 racks of pork baby back ribs (about 2-3 pounds each)
- Salt and pepper, to taste
- Your favorite BBQ rub or seasoning
- 2 cups BBQ sauce (homemade or store-bought)
- Optional: additional BBQ sauce for serving

Instructions:

1. Preheat your grill to indirect heat, aiming for a temperature of around 250°F to 275°F (120°C to 135°C). If using a charcoal grill, set up a two-zone fire by banking the coals to one side.
2. Prepare the ribs by removing the thin membrane from the back of each rack. Use a paper towel to grip the membrane and pull it off. This step helps tenderize the ribs and allows the flavors to penetrate better.
3. Season both sides of the ribs generously with salt, pepper, and your favorite BBQ rub or seasoning. Rub the seasoning into the meat, ensuring even coverage.
4. Place the seasoned ribs on the grill over indirect heat, bone side down. Close the lid and let them cook for about 2 to 2.5 hours, maintaining a consistent temperature.
5. After the first hour of cooking, you can optionally brush the ribs with some BBQ sauce. Continue cooking, basting occasionally with more BBQ sauce every 30 minutes or so.
6. Check the ribs for doneness by gently twisting a rib bone; if it starts to pull away from the meat easily, they're likely done. Another method is to use a meat thermometer to ensure the internal temperature reaches about 195°F to 203°F (90°C to 95°C).
7. Once the ribs are done, carefully remove them from the grill and transfer them to a cutting board. Let them rest for a few minutes before slicing.
8. Optionally, serve the ribs with extra BBQ sauce on the side for dipping or brushing onto the sliced ribs.
9. Serve your delicious BBQ ribs hot and enjoy the tender, flavorful meat that's perfect for any outdoor gathering or barbecue feast!

Grilled Corn on the Cob

Ingredients:

- 4 ears of fresh corn on the cob, husks intact
- Butter or olive oil, for brushing (optional)
- Salt and pepper, to taste
- Optional toppings: grated Parmesan cheese, chopped fresh herbs (such as parsley or cilantro), chili powder, lime wedges

Instructions:

1. Preheat your grill to medium-high heat.
2. Peel back the outer husks of the corn, but leave them attached at the base of the cob. Remove the silk (the fine threads) from the corn.
3. If desired, brush the corn with melted butter or olive oil for added flavor. Season with salt and pepper to taste.
4. Pull the husks back over the corn to cover them completely. This helps protect the corn from direct heat while allowing it to steam and cook inside the husks.
5. Place the corn on the preheated grill and cook for about 15-20 minutes, turning occasionally to ensure even cooking. The husks will become charred and slightly blackened, and the corn kernels will be tender.
6. Once the corn is cooked through, carefully remove it from the grill and let it cool for a few minutes.
7. To serve, peel back the husks and use them as handles, or remove them entirely. Optionally, brush the grilled corn with additional melted butter or olive oil, and sprinkle with grated Parmesan cheese, chopped fresh herbs, chili powder, or a squeeze of lime juice for extra flavor.
8. Serve the grilled corn on the cob hot as a delicious side dish or accompaniment to your favorite grilled meats or barbecue fare. Enjoy the smoky, sweet flavors of perfectly grilled corn!

Teriyaki Salmon Skewers

Ingredients:

- 1 pound salmon fillets, skin removed and cut into 1-inch cubes
- 1/4 cup soy sauce
- 2 tablespoons honey
- 1 tablespoon rice vinegar
- 1 tablespoon sesame oil
- 2 cloves garlic, minced
- 1 teaspoon grated fresh ginger
- 1 tablespoon cornstarch (optional, for thickening the marinade)
- Bamboo skewers, soaked in water for at least 30 minutes

Instructions:

1. In a bowl, whisk together the soy sauce, honey, rice vinegar, sesame oil, minced garlic, and grated ginger to make the teriyaki marinade. If you prefer a thicker marinade, you can whisk in a tablespoon of cornstarch.
2. Place the salmon cubes in a shallow dish or a resealable plastic bag. Pour the teriyaki marinade over the salmon, ensuring all pieces are coated. Cover or seal the dish/bag and refrigerate for at least 30 minutes to allow the flavors to develop.
3. While the salmon is marinating, preheat your grill to medium-high heat.
4. Thread the marinated salmon cubes onto the soaked bamboo skewers, leaving a small space between each piece.
5. Once the grill is hot, lightly oil the grates to prevent sticking. Place the salmon skewers on the grill, directly over the heat.
6. Grill the salmon skewers for about 3-4 minutes per side, or until the salmon is cooked through and slightly charred on the edges. Be careful not to overcook the salmon, as it can become dry.
7. While grilling, you can brush any leftover marinade onto the salmon skewers for added flavor, but discard any marinade that has come into contact with raw fish.
8. Once the salmon skewers are cooked to your liking, remove them from the grill and transfer to a serving platter.
9. Serve the teriyaki salmon skewers hot, garnished with sliced green onions or sesame seeds if desired. They pair well with steamed rice and grilled vegetables

for a complete meal. Enjoy the deliciously glazed and flavorful salmon skewers straight from the grill!

Tandoori Chicken

Ingredients:

- 4 bone-in, skin-on chicken thighs or drumsticks
- 1/2 cup plain yogurt
- 2 tablespoons lemon juice
- 2 tablespoons tandoori masala spice blend
- 1 tablespoon ginger paste or grated ginger
- 1 tablespoon garlic paste or minced garlic
- 1 teaspoon ground cumin
- 1 teaspoon ground coriander
- 1/2 teaspoon paprika (for color)
- 1/4 teaspoon cayenne pepper (adjust to taste for spice level)
- Salt, to taste
- Vegetable oil, for grilling

Instructions:

1. In a large bowl, combine the plain yogurt, lemon juice, tandoori masala spice blend, ginger paste, garlic paste, ground cumin, ground coriander, paprika, cayenne pepper, and salt. Mix well to form a smooth marinade.
2. Add the chicken thighs or drumsticks to the marinade, ensuring they are well coated. Cover the bowl with plastic wrap or transfer the chicken and marinade to a resealable plastic bag. Refrigerate for at least 4 hours or overnight to allow the flavors to penetrate the chicken.
3. Preheat your grill to medium-high heat.
4. Remove the chicken from the marinade and shake off any excess marinade. Discard the remaining marinade.
5. Lightly oil the grill grates to prevent sticking. Place the chicken pieces on the preheated grill, skin side down.
6. Grill the chicken for about 6-8 minutes per side, or until fully cooked and the internal temperature reaches 165°F (75°C). Cooking time may vary depending on the size and thickness of the chicken pieces.
7. During grilling, you can baste the chicken with a little vegetable oil or melted butter to keep it moist and enhance the flavor.

8. Once the chicken is cooked through and has developed a charred, slightly crispy exterior, remove it from the grill and transfer to a serving platter.
9. Let the tandoori chicken rest for a few minutes before serving to allow the juices to redistribute.
10. Serve the tandoori chicken hot, garnished with fresh cilantro and lemon wedges. It pairs well with naan bread, rice, or a side salad. Enjoy the aromatic and flavorful tandoori chicken straight from the grill!

Grilled Vegetable Kabobs

Ingredients:

- 2 bell peppers, cut into 1-inch pieces (any color)
- 2 zucchinis, sliced into rounds or half-moons
- 1 red onion, cut into 1-inch chunks
- 1 pint cherry tomatoes
- 8 ounces mushrooms, whole or halved
- 1/4 cup olive oil
- 2 tablespoons balsamic vinegar
- 2 cloves garlic, minced
- 1 teaspoon dried oregano
- 1 teaspoon dried basil
- Salt and pepper, to taste
- Wooden or metal skewers

Instructions:

1. If using wooden skewers, soak them in water for at least 30 minutes to prevent them from burning on the grill.
2. In a large bowl, whisk together the olive oil, balsamic vinegar, minced garlic, dried oregano, dried basil, salt, and pepper to make the marinade.
3. Add the bell peppers, zucchinis, red onion, cherry tomatoes, and mushrooms to the bowl with the marinade. Toss until all the vegetables are evenly coated. Let them marinate for at least 15-30 minutes to enhance the flavor.
4. Preheat your grill to medium-high heat.
5. Thread the marinated vegetables onto the skewers, alternating the different vegetables as desired.
6. Lightly oil the grill grates to prevent sticking. Place the vegetable skewers on the preheated grill.
7. Grill the vegetable kabobs for about 10-15 minutes, turning occasionally, or until the vegetables are tender and slightly charred.
8. Remove the vegetable skewers from the grill and transfer them to a serving platter.

9. Serve the grilled vegetable kabobs hot as a delicious and colorful side dish or vegetarian main course. Enjoy the smoky flavors and vibrant textures of grilled vegetables!

Spicy Grilled Shrimp

Ingredients:

- 1 pound large shrimp, peeled and deveined
- 2 tablespoons olive oil
- 2 cloves garlic, minced
- 1 teaspoon paprika
- 1/2 teaspoon cayenne pepper (adjust to taste)
- 1/2 teaspoon ground cumin
- 1/2 teaspoon dried oregano
- Salt and black pepper, to taste
- Lemon wedges, for serving
- Optional: chopped fresh cilantro or parsley for garnish

Instructions:

1. In a bowl, combine the olive oil, minced garlic, paprika, cayenne pepper, ground cumin, dried oregano, salt, and black pepper to make the marinade.
2. Add the peeled and deveined shrimp to the bowl with the marinade. Toss until the shrimp are evenly coated. Let them marinate for about 15-30 minutes to allow the flavors to develop.
3. Preheat your grill to medium-high heat.
4. Thread the marinated shrimp onto skewers, leaving a little space between each shrimp.
5. Lightly oil the grill grates to prevent sticking. Place the shrimp skewers on the preheated grill.
6. Grill the shrimp for about 2-3 minutes per side, or until they turn pink and opaque with grill marks.
7. Once the shrimp are cooked through, remove them from the grill and transfer them to a serving platter.
8. Serve the spicy grilled shrimp hot, garnished with lemon wedges and chopped fresh cilantro or parsley if desired. They make a flavorful appetizer or main course, perfect for any outdoor gathering or barbecue!

Garlic Butter Steak

Ingredients:

- 2 steaks of your choice (such as ribeye, New York strip, or sirloin), about 1 inch thick
- Salt and black pepper, to taste
- 2 tablespoons unsalted butter
- 4 cloves garlic, minced
- 1 tablespoon chopped fresh parsley (optional)
- Lemon wedges, for serving

Instructions:

1. Remove the steaks from the refrigerator and let them sit at room temperature for about 30 minutes to take the chill off.
2. Season both sides of the steaks generously with salt and black pepper.
3. Preheat your grill to high heat.
4. Once the grill is hot, lightly oil the grates to prevent sticking.
5. Place the seasoned steaks on the preheated grill. Cook for about 4-5 minutes on each side for medium-rare doneness, or adjust the cooking time according to your desired level of doneness and the thickness of the steaks.
6. While the steaks are grilling, prepare the garlic butter sauce. In a small saucepan or skillet, melt the butter over medium heat. Add the minced garlic and cook for 1-2 minutes, stirring frequently, until the garlic is fragrant and lightly golden. Remove from heat and stir in the chopped fresh parsley, if using.
7. Once the steaks are cooked to your liking, transfer them to a serving platter or individual plates.
8. Spoon the garlic butter sauce over the hot grilled steaks, allowing it to melt and coat the surface.
9. Let the steaks rest for a few minutes before serving to allow the juices to redistribute.
10. Serve the garlic butter steak hot, garnished with lemon wedges for squeezing over the steak before eating. Enjoy the succulent and flavorful steak with a rich garlic butter sauce straight from the grill!

Hawaiian Pork Chops

Ingredients:

- 4 boneless pork chops
- 1/2 cup pineapple juice
- 1/4 cup soy sauce
- 2 tablespoons brown sugar
- 2 cloves garlic, minced
- 1 teaspoon grated fresh ginger
- 1/4 teaspoon black pepper
- 1/4 teaspoon red pepper flakes (optional, for heat)
- 1 tablespoon vegetable oil (for grilling)
- Pineapple slices, for serving (optional)
- Chopped fresh cilantro or green onions, for garnish (optional)

Instructions:

1. In a bowl, whisk together the pineapple juice, soy sauce, brown sugar, minced garlic, grated ginger, black pepper, and red pepper flakes (if using) to make the marinade.
2. Place the pork chops in a shallow dish or a resealable plastic bag. Pour the marinade over the pork chops, ensuring they are well coated. Cover the dish or seal the bag and refrigerate for at least 30 minutes to allow the flavors to meld.
3. Preheat your grill to medium-high heat.
4. Remove the pork chops from the marinade and discard any excess marinade.
5. Lightly oil the grill grates to prevent sticking. Place the pork chops on the preheated grill.
6. Grill the pork chops for about 4-5 minutes per side, or until they are cooked through and have reached an internal temperature of 145°F (63°C). Cooking time may vary depending on the thickness of the pork chops.
7. While grilling, you can brush any remaining marinade onto the pork chops for added flavor, but discard any marinade that has come into contact with raw meat.
8. Once the pork chops are cooked through, remove them from the grill and transfer them to a serving platter.

9. Optionally, serve the grilled Hawaiian pork chops with pineapple slices for an extra tropical touch.
10. Garnish the pork chops with chopped fresh cilantro or green onions if desired, and serve hot. Enjoy the sweet and savory flavors of these delicious Hawaiian-inspired pork chops!

Chimichurri Grilled Lamb Chops

Ingredients:

For the lamb chops:

- 8 lamb loin chops
- Salt and black pepper, to taste

For the chimichurri sauce:

- 1 cup fresh parsley leaves, finely chopped
- 1/4 cup fresh cilantro leaves, finely chopped
- 3 cloves garlic, minced
- 1/4 cup red wine vinegar
- 1/2 cup extra virgin olive oil
- 1 tablespoon dried oregano
- 1 teaspoon red pepper flakes (adjust to taste)
- Salt and black pepper, to taste
- Optional: lemon wedges, for serving

Instructions:

1. Preheat your grill to medium-high heat.
2. Season the lamb chops generously with salt and black pepper on both sides.
3. In a small bowl, prepare the chimichurri sauce by combining the finely chopped parsley, cilantro, minced garlic, red wine vinegar, extra virgin olive oil, dried oregano, and red pepper flakes. Season with salt and black pepper to taste. Mix well to combine.
4. Set aside a portion of the chimichurri sauce for serving, and use the remaining sauce to marinate the lamb chops. Place the lamb chops in a shallow dish or resealable plastic bag, and pour the chimichurri sauce over them. Ensure that all the chops are coated evenly with the marinade. Cover the dish or seal the bag, and refrigerate for at least 30 minutes to allow the flavors to meld.
5. Once the grill is hot, lightly oil the grates to prevent sticking.
6. Remove the lamb chops from the marinade and discard any excess marinade.

7. Place the lamb chops on the preheated grill and cook for about 3-4 minutes per side for medium-rare, or adjust the cooking time according to your preferred level of doneness and the thickness of the chops.
8. While grilling, you can brush the lamb chops with a little extra chimichurri sauce for added flavor, if desired.
9. Once the lamb chops are cooked to your liking, remove them from the grill and transfer them to a serving platter.
10. Serve the grilled chimichurri lamb chops hot, garnished with a drizzle of the reserved chimichurri sauce and lemon wedges on the side. Enjoy the succulent and flavorful lamb chops with the vibrant and herbaceous chimichurri sauce!

Grilled Portobello Mushrooms

Ingredients:

- 4 large portobello mushrooms
- 1/4 cup balsamic vinegar
- 2 tablespoons olive oil
- 2 cloves garlic, minced
- 1 teaspoon dried thyme
- Salt and black pepper, to taste
- Optional toppings: crumbled goat cheese, chopped fresh parsley, balsamic glaze

Instructions:

1. Clean the portobello mushrooms by gently wiping them with a damp paper towel to remove any dirt. Remove the stems and discard them, or save them for another use.
2. In a shallow dish or a resealable plastic bag, combine the balsamic vinegar, olive oil, minced garlic, dried thyme, salt, and black pepper to make the marinade.
3. Place the portobello mushrooms in the marinade, gill side down, and let them marinate for about 15-30 minutes, turning occasionally to ensure even coating.
4. Preheat your grill to medium-high heat.
5. Once the grill is hot, lightly oil the grates to prevent sticking.
6. Place the marinated portobello mushrooms on the preheated grill, gill side down. Reserve the marinade for basting.
7. Grill the mushrooms for about 4-5 minutes on each side, or until they are tender and have grill marks.
8. During grilling, you can baste the mushrooms with the reserved marinade for added flavor.
9. Once the mushrooms are cooked through, remove them from the grill and transfer them to a serving platter.
10. Optionally, top the grilled portobello mushrooms with crumbled goat cheese, chopped fresh parsley, and a drizzle of balsamic glaze before serving.
11. Serve the grilled portobello mushrooms hot as a delicious vegetarian main course or side dish. Enjoy their meaty texture and savory flavor straight from the grill!

Cajun Grilled Tilapia

Ingredients:

- 4 tilapia fillets
- 2 tablespoons olive oil
- 1 tablespoon Cajun seasoning
- 1 teaspoon paprika
- 1/2 teaspoon garlic powder
- 1/2 teaspoon onion powder
- 1/4 teaspoon cayenne pepper (adjust to taste for spice level)
- Salt and black pepper, to taste
- Lemon wedges, for serving
- Chopped fresh parsley, for garnish (optional)

Instructions:

1. Preheat your grill to medium-high heat.
2. In a small bowl, combine the olive oil, Cajun seasoning, paprika, garlic powder, onion powder, cayenne pepper, salt, and black pepper to make the Cajun seasoning blend.
3. Pat the tilapia fillets dry with paper towels. Brush both sides of each fillet with the Cajun seasoning blend, ensuring they are evenly coated.
4. Once the grill is hot, lightly oil the grates to prevent sticking.
5. Place the seasoned tilapia fillets on the preheated grill.
6. Grill the tilapia for about 3-4 minutes per side, or until they are cooked through and easily flake with a fork. Cooking time may vary depending on the thickness of the fillets.
7. While grilling, you can optionally brush the tilapia fillets with a little extra olive oil or melted butter for added moisture and flavor.
8. Once the tilapia is cooked, remove it from the grill and transfer it to a serving platter.
9. Garnish the grilled Cajun tilapia with chopped fresh parsley and serve with lemon wedges on the side for squeezing over the fish before eating.
10. Serve the tilapia hot as a delicious and flavorful seafood dish. Enjoy the spicy Cajun seasoning and tender, flaky texture of the grilled tilapia!

Honey Mustard Grilled Chicken

Ingredients:

- 4 boneless, skinless chicken breasts
- Salt and black pepper, to taste
- 1/4 cup honey
- 2 tablespoons Dijon mustard
- 2 tablespoons whole grain mustard
- 2 tablespoons olive oil
- 2 cloves garlic, minced
- 1 tablespoon apple cider vinegar
- Optional: chopped fresh herbs (such as parsley or thyme) for garnish

Instructions:

1. Preheat your grill to medium-high heat.
2. Season the chicken breasts with salt and black pepper on both sides.
3. In a bowl, whisk together the honey, Dijon mustard, whole grain mustard, olive oil, minced garlic, and apple cider vinegar to make the honey mustard marinade.
4. Place the seasoned chicken breasts in a shallow dish or resealable plastic bag. Pour the honey mustard marinade over the chicken, ensuring it is well coated. Cover the dish or seal the bag, and refrigerate for at least 30 minutes to allow the flavors to meld.
5. Once the grill is hot, lightly oil the grates to prevent sticking.
6. Remove the chicken breasts from the marinade and discard any excess marinade.
7. Place the chicken breasts on the preheated grill. Grill for about 6-8 minutes per side, or until they are cooked through and reach an internal temperature of 165°F (75°C). Cooking time may vary depending on the thickness of the chicken breasts.
8. While grilling, you can baste the chicken breasts with any remaining marinade for added flavor.
9. Once the chicken is cooked through, remove it from the grill and transfer it to a serving platter.
10. Optionally, garnish the grilled honey mustard chicken with chopped fresh herbs for a pop of color and flavor.

11. Serve the chicken hot as a delicious and flavorful main course. Enjoy the sweet and tangy taste of the honey mustard marinade paired with juicy grilled chicken breasts!

Mediterranean Grilled Eggplant

Ingredients:

- 2 large eggplants, sliced into 1/2-inch rounds
- Salt, for sprinkling
- 1/4 cup olive oil
- 2 cloves garlic, minced
- 1 teaspoon dried oregano
- 1/2 teaspoon dried thyme
- 1/2 teaspoon paprika
- 1/4 teaspoon black pepper
- Juice of 1 lemon
- Optional toppings: crumbled feta cheese, chopped fresh parsley, chopped Kalamata olives

Instructions:

1. Place the eggplant slices on a baking sheet lined with paper towels. Sprinkle salt over both sides of the eggplant slices and let them sit for about 15-20 minutes. This helps draw out excess moisture and bitterness from the eggplant.
2. Meanwhile, preheat your grill to medium-high heat.
3. After the eggplant slices have rested, pat them dry with paper towels to remove the excess moisture and salt.
4. In a small bowl, whisk together the olive oil, minced garlic, dried oregano, dried thyme, paprika, black pepper, and lemon juice to make the marinade.
5. Brush both sides of each eggplant slice with the marinade, ensuring they are evenly coated.
6. Once the grill is hot, lightly oil the grates to prevent sticking.
7. Place the marinated eggplant slices on the preheated grill. Grill for about 3-4 minutes per side, or until they are tender and have grill marks.
8. While grilling, you can brush the eggplant slices with any remaining marinade for added flavor.
9. Once the eggplant is cooked through and has developed a nice char, remove it from the grill and transfer it to a serving platter.

10. Optionally, top the grilled Mediterranean eggplant slices with crumbled feta cheese, chopped fresh parsley, and chopped Kalamata olives for extra flavor and Mediterranean flair.
11. Serve the grilled eggplant hot as a delicious and nutritious side dish or appetizer. Enjoy the smoky flavors and tender texture of the Mediterranean-inspired grilled eggplant!

Korean BBQ Beef

Ingredients:

- 1 pound beef sirloin or ribeye, thinly sliced
- 1/4 cup soy sauce
- 2 tablespoons brown sugar
- 2 tablespoons rice vinegar
- 2 tablespoons sesame oil
- 4 cloves garlic, minced
- 1 tablespoon grated fresh ginger
- 2 green onions, chopped (plus extra for garnish)
- 1 tablespoon sesame seeds (optional, for garnish)
- 1/4 teaspoon black pepper
- 1/4 teaspoon red pepper flakes (adjust to taste for spice level)
- Vegetable oil, for grilling

Instructions:

1. In a bowl, whisk together the soy sauce, brown sugar, rice vinegar, sesame oil, minced garlic, grated ginger, chopped green onions, black pepper, and red pepper flakes to make the marinade.
2. Place the thinly sliced beef in a shallow dish or a resealable plastic bag. Pour the marinade over the beef, ensuring all pieces are well coated. Cover the dish or seal the bag, and refrigerate for at least 30 minutes to allow the flavors to meld.
3. Preheat your grill to medium-high heat.
4. Remove the marinated beef from the refrigerator and let it sit at room temperature for about 10-15 minutes.
5. Once the grill is hot, lightly oil the grates to prevent sticking.
6. Thread the marinated beef slices onto skewers, if desired, or you can grill them directly on the grates.
7. Grill the beef skewers or slices for about 2-3 minutes per side, or until they are cooked through and have a nice char.
8. While grilling, you can brush any remaining marinade onto the beef for added flavor, but discard any marinade that has come into contact with raw meat.
9. Once the beef is cooked, remove it from the grill and transfer it to a serving platter.

10. Garnish the Korean BBQ beef with chopped green onions and sesame seeds, if desired.
11. Serve the grilled Korean BBQ beef hot, accompanied by steamed rice and your favorite side dishes such as kimchi or pickled vegetables. Enjoy the savory, sweet, and slightly spicy flavors of this delicious Korean-inspired dish!

Lemon Herb Grilled Swordfish

Ingredients:

- 4 swordfish steaks (about 6 ounces each)
- Salt and black pepper, to taste
- 1/4 cup olive oil
- 2 tablespoons lemon juice
- 2 cloves garlic, minced
- 1 tablespoon chopped fresh parsley
- 1 tablespoon chopped fresh basil
- 1 teaspoon chopped fresh thyme
- 1 teaspoon grated lemon zest
- Lemon wedges, for serving

Instructions:

1. Preheat your grill to medium-high heat.
2. Season the swordfish steaks with salt and black pepper on both sides.
3. In a small bowl, whisk together the olive oil, lemon juice, minced garlic, chopped fresh parsley, chopped fresh basil, chopped fresh thyme, and grated lemon zest to make the marinade.
4. Place the swordfish steaks in a shallow dish or a resealable plastic bag. Pour the marinade over the swordfish, ensuring they are well coated. Cover the dish or seal the bag, and refrigerate for at least 30 minutes to allow the flavors to meld.
5. Once the grill is hot, lightly oil the grates to prevent sticking.
6. Remove the swordfish steaks from the marinade and discard any excess marinade.
7. Place the swordfish steaks on the preheated grill. Grill for about 3-4 minutes per side, or until they are cooked through and have grill marks. Cooking time may vary depending on the thickness of the swordfish steaks.
8. While grilling, you can baste the swordfish steaks with any remaining marinade for added flavor.
9. Once the swordfish is cooked through and flakes easily with a fork, remove it from the grill and transfer it to a serving platter.
10. Serve the grilled lemon herb swordfish hot, garnished with lemon wedges for squeezing over the fish before eating.

11. Enjoy the fresh and vibrant flavors of the lemon and herbs combined with the tender and succulent swordfish straight from the grill!

Chipotle Lime Grilled Corn

Ingredients:

- 4 ears of corn, husks removed
- 2 tablespoons unsalted butter, melted
- 1 tablespoon chipotle chili powder
- 1 teaspoon ground cumin
- Zest and juice of 1 lime
- Salt, to taste
- Chopped fresh cilantro, for garnish (optional)
- Lime wedges, for serving

Instructions:

1. Preheat your grill to medium-high heat.
2. In a small bowl, combine the melted butter, chipotle chili powder, ground cumin, lime zest, lime juice, and salt. Mix well to make the chipotle lime seasoning.
3. Place the ears of corn on the preheated grill. Grill for about 10-12 minutes, turning occasionally, or until the corn is cooked through and lightly charred in spots.
4. While grilling, brush the corn with the chipotle lime seasoning, turning occasionally to ensure all sides are coated evenly. Continue grilling until the corn is tender and the seasoning has caramelized slightly.
5. Once the corn is grilled to your liking, remove it from the grill and transfer it to a serving platter.
6. Optionally, sprinkle the grilled corn with chopped fresh cilantro for an extra burst of flavor.
7. Serve the chipotle lime grilled corn hot, accompanied by lime wedges for squeezing over the corn before eating. Enjoy the smoky, spicy, and tangy flavors of this delicious grilled corn!

Jamaican Jerk Chicken

Ingredients:

- 4 chicken quarters (legs and thighs), skin-on and bone-in
- 1/4 cup soy sauce
- 3 tablespoons olive oil
- 3 tablespoons brown sugar
- 2 tablespoons lime juice
- 2 tablespoons apple cider vinegar
- 4 cloves garlic, minced
- 2 tablespoons fresh thyme leaves, chopped
- 2 tablespoons fresh ginger, grated
- 2 tablespoons ground allspice
- 1 tablespoon ground black pepper
- 1 tablespoon paprika
- 1 tablespoon dried crushed red pepper flakes (adjust to taste)
- 1 teaspoon ground cinnamon
- 1 teaspoon ground nutmeg
- Salt, to taste
- Optional: sliced scotch bonnet peppers or habanero peppers for extra heat

Instructions:

1. In a large bowl, combine the soy sauce, olive oil, brown sugar, lime juice, apple cider vinegar, minced garlic, chopped thyme leaves, grated ginger, ground allspice, ground black pepper, paprika, crushed red pepper flakes, ground cinnamon, and ground nutmeg to make the jerk marinade. Mix well to combine.
2. Score the chicken quarters with shallow cuts to help the marinade penetrate.
3. Place the chicken quarters in a shallow dish or a resealable plastic bag. Pour the jerk marinade over the chicken, ensuring all pieces are well coated. Cover the dish or seal the bag, and refrigerate for at least 4 hours or overnight to allow the flavors to meld.
4. Preheat your grill to medium-high heat.
5. Once the grill is hot, lightly oil the grates to prevent sticking.
6. Remove the chicken quarters from the marinade and discard any excess marinade.

7. Place the chicken quarters on the preheated grill, skin-side down. Grill for about 5-6 minutes on each side, or until the chicken is cooked through and has developed a charred and crispy exterior.
8. While grilling, you can baste the chicken quarters with any remaining marinade for added flavor.
9. Once the chicken is cooked through and reaches an internal temperature of 165°F (75°C), remove it from the grill and transfer it to a serving platter.
10. Serve the Jamaican jerk chicken hot, accompanied by rice and peas, fried plantains, or your favorite Caribbean side dishes. Enjoy the bold and spicy flavors of this classic Jamaican dish!

Maple Glazed Grilled Salmon

Ingredients:

- 4 salmon fillets, skin-on or skinless (about 6 ounces each)
- Salt and black pepper, to taste
- 1/4 cup maple syrup
- 2 tablespoons soy sauce
- 2 tablespoons olive oil
- 2 cloves garlic, minced
- 1 tablespoon Dijon mustard
- 1 tablespoon apple cider vinegar
- Optional: chopped fresh herbs (such as parsley or dill) for garnish

Instructions:

1. Preheat your grill to medium-high heat.
2. Season the salmon fillets with salt and black pepper on both sides.
3. In a small bowl, whisk together the maple syrup, soy sauce, olive oil, minced garlic, Dijon mustard, and apple cider vinegar to make the maple glaze.
4. Place the salmon fillets in a shallow dish or a resealable plastic bag. Pour half of the maple glaze over the salmon, reserving the other half for later. Ensure that the salmon fillets are well coated with the glaze. Cover the dish or seal the bag, and let the salmon marinate for about 15-30 minutes in the refrigerator.
5. Once the grill is hot, lightly oil the grates to prevent sticking.
6. Place the marinated salmon fillets on the preheated grill, skin-side down if applicable. Reserve any excess marinade for basting.
7. Grill the salmon for about 4-5 minutes per side, depending on the thickness of the fillets, or until the salmon is cooked through and flakes easily with a fork. During grilling, you can brush the salmon with the reserved marinade for extra flavor.
8. Once the salmon is cooked to your liking, remove it from the grill and transfer it to a serving platter.
9. Optionally, garnish the maple glazed grilled salmon with chopped fresh herbs for added freshness and color.
10. Serve the grilled salmon hot, accompanied by your favorite side dishes such as roasted vegetables, rice, or a salad. Enjoy the sweet and savory flavors of this delicious maple glazed salmon straight from the grill!

Thai Peanut Grilled Tofu

Ingredients:

- 1 block (14-16 ounces) extra firm tofu, pressed and drained
- 1/4 cup creamy peanut butter
- 2 tablespoons soy sauce
- 2 tablespoons lime juice
- 2 tablespoons maple syrup or honey
- 2 cloves garlic, minced
- 1 tablespoon grated fresh ginger
- 1 tablespoon sesame oil
- 1 tablespoon sriracha sauce (adjust to taste)
- 2 tablespoons chopped fresh cilantro (plus extra for garnish)
- Optional: crushed peanuts, sliced green onions, lime wedges for serving

Instructions:

1. Preheat your grill to medium-high heat.
2. Slice the pressed and drained tofu block into thick slabs, about 1/2 inch to 3/4 inch thick.
3. In a bowl, whisk together the creamy peanut butter, soy sauce, lime juice, maple syrup or honey, minced garlic, grated ginger, sesame oil, and sriracha sauce until smooth and well combined.
4. Stir in the chopped fresh cilantro into the peanut sauce.
5. Place the tofu slabs in a shallow dish or a resealable plastic bag. Pour half of the peanut sauce over the tofu, reserving the other half for later. Ensure that the tofu slabs are well coated with the sauce. Cover the dish or seal the bag, and let the tofu marinate for about 15-30 minutes in the refrigerator.
6. Once the grill is hot, lightly oil the grates to prevent sticking.
7. Place the marinated tofu slabs on the preheated grill. Grill for about 3-4 minutes on each side, or until the tofu is lightly charred and heated through.
8. During grilling, you can brush the tofu with the reserved peanut sauce for extra flavor.
9. Once the tofu is grilled to your liking, remove it from the grill and transfer it to a serving platter.
10. Optionally, garnish the Thai peanut grilled tofu with crushed peanuts, sliced green onions, and additional chopped cilantro for extra texture and flavor.

11. Serve the grilled tofu hot, accompanied by rice or noodles and your favorite vegetables. Squeeze fresh lime juice over the tofu before serving for a burst of citrusy freshness. Enjoy the delicious Thai-inspired flavors of this grilled tofu dish!

Bourbon BBQ Pork Tenderloin

Ingredients:

- 2 pork tenderloins (about 1 pound each)
- Salt and black pepper, to taste
- 1/4 cup bourbon
- 1/4 cup ketchup
- 2 tablespoons soy sauce
- 2 tablespoons Worcestershire sauce
- 2 tablespoons brown sugar
- 1 tablespoon Dijon mustard
- 2 cloves garlic, minced
- 1 teaspoon smoked paprika
- 1/2 teaspoon onion powder
- 1/2 teaspoon garlic powder
- Vegetable oil, for grilling

Instructions:

1. Preheat your grill to medium-high heat.
2. Season the pork tenderloins with salt and black pepper on all sides.
3. In a bowl, whisk together the bourbon, ketchup, soy sauce, Worcestershire sauce, brown sugar, Dijon mustard, minced garlic, smoked paprika, onion powder, and garlic powder to make the bourbon BBQ marinade.
4. Place the pork tenderloins in a shallow dish or a resealable plastic bag. Pour the marinade over the pork, ensuring they are well coated. Cover the dish or seal the bag, and let the pork marinate for about 30 minutes to 1 hour in the refrigerator.
5. Once the grill is hot, lightly oil the grates to prevent sticking.
6. Remove the pork tenderloins from the marinade and discard any excess marinade.
7. Place the pork tenderloins on the preheated grill. Grill for about 15-20 minutes, turning occasionally, or until the pork is cooked through and reaches an internal temperature of 145°F (63°C). Cooking time may vary depending on the thickness of the tenderloins.
8. While grilling, you can brush the pork tenderloins with any remaining marinade for added flavor.

9. Once the pork is cooked through, remove it from the grill and transfer it to a cutting board. Let it rest for a few minutes before slicing.
10. Slice the bourbon BBQ pork tenderloins into thick slices and serve hot. Enjoy the tender and flavorful pork with a hint of smokiness from the grill and the rich bourbon BBQ sauce!

Grilled Stuffed Bell Peppers

Ingredients:

- 4 large bell peppers (any color), halved and seeds removed
- 1 cup cooked quinoa or rice
- 1 cup cooked black beans, drained and rinsed
- 1 cup corn kernels (fresh, canned, or frozen)
- 1 cup diced tomatoes
- 1/2 cup diced onion
- 2 cloves garlic, minced
- 1 teaspoon ground cumin
- 1 teaspoon chili powder
- Salt and black pepper, to taste
- 1 cup shredded cheese (such as cheddar, Monterey Jack, or a blend)
- Optional toppings: chopped fresh cilantro, sliced green onions, sour cream, salsa

Instructions:

1. Preheat your grill to medium-high heat.
2. In a large bowl, combine the cooked quinoa or rice, black beans, corn kernels, diced tomatoes, diced onion, minced garlic, ground cumin, chili powder, salt, and black pepper. Mix well to combine.
3. Fill each bell pepper half with the quinoa or rice mixture, pressing it down gently to pack it in.
4. Sprinkle shredded cheese over the stuffed bell peppers.
5. Place the stuffed bell peppers on the preheated grill, cover, and cook for about 15-20 minutes, or until the peppers are tender and the filling is heated through.
6. While grilling, you can cover the grill to help melt the cheese and cook the peppers evenly.
7. Once the stuffed bell peppers are cooked through and the cheese is melted and bubbly, remove them from the grill and transfer them to a serving platter.
8. Optionally, garnish the grilled stuffed bell peppers with chopped fresh cilantro, sliced green onions, and serve with sour cream and salsa on the side.
9. Serve the grilled stuffed bell peppers hot as a delicious and satisfying vegetarian main course or side dish. Enjoy the flavorful and nutritious combination of quinoa or rice, beans, vegetables, and melted cheese!

Garlic Rosemary Lamb Kebabs

Ingredients:

- 1 1/2 pounds boneless lamb, cut into 1-inch cubes
- 1/4 cup olive oil
- 4 cloves garlic, minced
- 2 tablespoons chopped fresh rosemary leaves
- 1 tablespoon lemon juice
- 1 teaspoon lemon zest
- Salt and black pepper, to taste
- Cherry tomatoes, red onion chunks, and bell pepper chunks for skewering (optional)

Instructions:

1. If using wooden skewers, soak them in water for about 30 minutes to prevent burning.
2. In a large bowl, combine the olive oil, minced garlic, chopped rosemary leaves, lemon juice, lemon zest, salt, and black pepper. Mix well to create the marinade.
3. Add the lamb cubes to the marinade and toss to coat them evenly. Cover the bowl with plastic wrap or transfer the lamb and marinade to a resealable plastic bag. Refrigerate and marinate for at least 1 hour, or up to overnight.
4. Preheat your grill to medium-high heat.
5. Thread the marinated lamb cubes onto the skewers, alternating with cherry tomatoes, red onion chunks, and bell pepper chunks if desired.
6. Lightly oil the grill grates to prevent sticking.
7. Place the lamb kebabs on the preheated grill and cook for about 8-10 minutes, turning occasionally, or until the lamb is cooked to your desired level of doneness and has a nice char on the outside.
8. Once cooked, remove the lamb kebabs from the grill and let them rest for a few minutes before serving.
9. Serve the garlic rosemary lamb kebabs hot, garnished with additional fresh rosemary leaves if desired. Enjoy the flavorful combination of tender lamb infused with garlic and rosemary straight from the grill!

Chili Lime Grilled Chicken Wings

Ingredients:

- 2 pounds chicken wings, separated into flats and drumettes
- 1/4 cup olive oil
- 2 tablespoons lime juice
- Zest of 1 lime
- 2 cloves garlic, minced
- 1 teaspoon chili powder
- 1/2 teaspoon paprika
- 1/2 teaspoon ground cumin
- 1/2 teaspoon ground coriander
- 1/4 teaspoon cayenne pepper (adjust to taste)
- Salt and black pepper, to taste
- Lime wedges, for serving
- Chopped fresh cilantro, for garnish (optional)

Instructions:

1. In a bowl, whisk together the olive oil, lime juice, lime zest, minced garlic, chili powder, paprika, ground cumin, ground coriander, cayenne pepper, salt, and black pepper to make the marinade.
2. Place the chicken wings in a large resealable plastic bag or a shallow dish. Pour the marinade over the chicken wings, ensuring they are evenly coated. Seal the bag or cover the dish, and refrigerate for at least 1 hour, or up to overnight, to allow the flavors to meld.
3. Preheat your grill to medium-high heat.
4. Remove the chicken wings from the marinade and discard any excess marinade.
5. Lightly oil the grill grates to prevent sticking.
6. Place the chicken wings on the preheated grill and cook for about 20-25 minutes, turning occasionally, or until they are cooked through and have crispy, charred edges.
7. While grilling, you can brush the chicken wings with any remaining marinade for added flavor.
8. Once the chicken wings are cooked through and crispy, remove them from the grill and transfer them to a serving platter.

9. Serve the chili lime grilled chicken wings hot, garnished with lime wedges and chopped fresh cilantro if desired. Enjoy the zesty and spicy flavors of these delicious grilled chicken wings!

Grilled Veggie Quesadillas

Ingredients:

- 4 large flour tortillas
- 1 cup shredded cheese (cheddar, Monterey Jack, or a blend)
- 1 cup grilled vegetables (such as bell peppers, onions, zucchini, mushrooms, or corn)
- 1/2 cup black beans, drained and rinsed (optional)
- 1/4 cup chopped fresh cilantro (optional)
- Olive oil or cooking spray, for grilling

Instructions:

1. Preheat your grill to medium heat.
2. Place one tortilla on a flat surface. Sprinkle half of the shredded cheese evenly over one half of the tortilla.
3. Layer half of the grilled vegetables and black beans (if using) over the cheese.
4. Sprinkle chopped cilantro (if using) over the vegetables.
5. Sprinkle the remaining shredded cheese over the vegetables.
6. Fold the tortilla in half to cover the filling, creating a half-moon shape.
7. Repeat the process with the remaining tortillas and filling ingredients.
8. Lightly brush olive oil or spray cooking spray on both sides of each quesadilla.
9. Place the quesadillas directly on the grill grates and cook for 2-3 minutes per side, or until the tortillas are crispy and golden brown and the cheese is melted.
10. Use a spatula to carefully flip the quesadillas halfway through cooking.
11. Once the quesadillas are grilled to perfection, remove them from the grill and transfer them to a cutting board.
12. Let the quesadillas rest for a minute or two before slicing them into wedges.
13. Serve the grilled veggie quesadillas hot, accompanied by salsa, guacamole, or sour cream for dipping, if desired. Enjoy the delicious combination of grilled vegetables and melted cheese in a crispy tortilla shell!

Bacon Wrapped BBQ Shrimp

Ingredients:

- 12 large shrimp, peeled and deveined, tails left on
- 6 slices bacon, cut in half crosswise
- 1/4 cup barbecue sauce
- 1 tablespoon honey
- 1 teaspoon smoked paprika
- 1/2 teaspoon garlic powder
- 1/4 teaspoon cayenne pepper (optional, for added heat)
- Salt and black pepper, to taste
- Wooden toothpicks, soaked in water for 30 minutes

Instructions:

1. Preheat your grill to medium-high heat.
2. In a small bowl, whisk together the barbecue sauce, honey, smoked paprika, garlic powder, cayenne pepper (if using), salt, and black pepper to make the BBQ sauce mixture.
3. Wrap each shrimp with a half slice of bacon and secure it with a wooden toothpick, threading the toothpick through the bacon and shrimp to hold them together.
4. Brush both sides of the bacon-wrapped shrimp with the BBQ sauce mixture, ensuring they are well coated.
5. Once the grill is hot, lightly oil the grates to prevent sticking.
6. Place the bacon-wrapped shrimp on the preheated grill. Grill for about 2-3 minutes on each side, or until the bacon is crispy and the shrimp is cooked through and pink.
7. While grilling, you can brush the shrimp with any remaining BBQ sauce mixture for added flavor.
8. Once the bacon-wrapped shrimp are cooked to perfection, remove them from the grill and transfer them to a serving platter.
9. Serve the bacon-wrapped BBQ shrimp hot as a delicious appetizer or main dish. Enjoy the smoky, savory, and slightly sweet flavors of these irresistible grilled shrimp!

Teriyaki Beef Skewers

Ingredients:

- 1 pound beef sirloin or flank steak, thinly sliced against the grain
- 1/4 cup soy sauce
- 2 tablespoons honey or brown sugar
- 2 tablespoons mirin (Japanese rice wine) or dry sherry
- 2 cloves garlic, minced
- 1 teaspoon grated fresh ginger
- 1 tablespoon sesame oil
- 1 tablespoon vegetable oil, for grilling
- Wooden skewers, soaked in water for 30 minutes

Instructions:

1. In a bowl, whisk together the soy sauce, honey or brown sugar, mirin or dry sherry, minced garlic, grated ginger, and sesame oil to make the teriyaki marinade.
2. Place the thinly sliced beef in a shallow dish or a resealable plastic bag. Pour the teriyaki marinade over the beef, ensuring all pieces are well coated. Cover the dish or seal the bag, and refrigerate for at least 30 minutes to 1 hour, allowing the flavors to meld.
3. Preheat your grill to medium-high heat.
4. Remove the beef from the marinade and discard any excess marinade.
5. Thread the marinated beef slices onto the soaked wooden skewers, folding the slices back and forth as needed to create a zigzag pattern on the skewers.
6. Lightly oil the grill grates to prevent sticking.
7. Place the beef skewers on the preheated grill. Grill for about 2-3 minutes on each side, or until the beef is cooked to your desired level of doneness and has a nice char.
8. While grilling, you can brush the beef skewers with any remaining marinade for added flavor.
9. Once the beef skewers are cooked to perfection, remove them from the grill and transfer them to a serving platter.
10. Serve the teriyaki beef skewers hot as a delicious appetizer or main dish. Enjoy the savory, sweet, and slightly tangy flavors of these irresistible grilled beef skewers!

Grilled Caesar Salad

Ingredients:

- 2 hearts of romaine lettuce, halved lengthwise
- Olive oil, for brushing
- Salt and black pepper, to taste
- Caesar salad dressing (store-bought or homemade)
- Shredded Parmesan cheese, for garnish
- Croutons, for garnish (optional)
- Lemon wedges, for serving

Instructions:

1. Preheat your grill to medium-high heat.
2. Brush the cut sides of the romaine lettuce halves with olive oil and season with salt and black pepper.
3. Place the romaine lettuce halves, cut side down, on the preheated grill. Grill for about 1-2 minutes, or until they have grill marks and are slightly charred.
4. Carefully flip the romaine lettuce halves using tongs and grill for an additional 1-2 minutes on the other side.
5. Remove the grilled romaine lettuce halves from the grill and transfer them to a serving platter or individual plates.
6. Drizzle Caesar salad dressing over the grilled romaine lettuce halves, ensuring they are evenly coated.
7. Sprinkle shredded Parmesan cheese over the grilled romaine lettuce halves.
8. Optionally, garnish with croutons for added crunch and texture.
9. Serve the grilled Caesar salad immediately, accompanied by lemon wedges for squeezing over the lettuce just before eating.
10. Enjoy the smoky, charred flavor of the grilled romaine lettuce combined with the creamy Caesar dressing and tangy Parmesan cheese!

Pineapple Rum Glazed Ham

Ingredients:

- 1 bone-in ham (about 6-8 pounds)
- 1 cup pineapple juice
- 1/2 cup brown sugar
- 1/4 cup dark rum
- 1/4 cup honey
- 2 tablespoons Dijon mustard
- 2 cloves garlic, minced
- 1 teaspoon ground ginger
- 1/2 teaspoon ground cloves
- Pineapple slices and maraschino cherries, for garnish

Instructions:

1. Preheat your oven to 325°F (160°C).
2. Place the ham in a large roasting pan, cut side down.
3. Score the surface of the ham with shallow cuts in a diamond pattern, making sure not to cut too deeply into the meat.
4. In a saucepan, combine the pineapple juice, brown sugar, dark rum, honey, Dijon mustard, minced garlic, ground ginger, and ground cloves. Bring the mixture to a simmer over medium heat, stirring occasionally, until the brown sugar is dissolved and the glaze is slightly thickened, about 5-7 minutes.
5. Pour about half of the pineapple rum glaze over the ham, making sure to coat it evenly.
6. Cover the ham loosely with aluminum foil and roast in the preheated oven for about 1 1/2 to 2 hours, or until the internal temperature reaches 140°F (60°C), basting with the remaining glaze every 30 minutes.
7. About 30 minutes before the ham is done, remove the foil to allow the surface to caramelize and develop a golden-brown color.
8. Once the ham is cooked through and has a caramelized glaze, remove it from the oven and let it rest for about 10-15 minutes before slicing.
9. Transfer the sliced ham to a serving platter and garnish with pineapple slices and maraschino cherries, if desired.

10. Serve the pineapple rum glazed ham hot or at room temperature, accompanied by your favorite side dishes. Enjoy the sweet and savory flavors of this delicious holiday centerpiece!

Moroccan Spiced Grilled Chicken

Ingredients:

- 4 boneless, skinless chicken breasts
- 2 tablespoons olive oil
- 2 cloves garlic, minced
- 1 teaspoon ground cumin
- 1 teaspoon ground coriander
- 1 teaspoon ground paprika
- 1/2 teaspoon ground cinnamon
- 1/2 teaspoon ground ginger
- 1/2 teaspoon ground turmeric
- 1/4 teaspoon cayenne pepper (adjust to taste)
- Salt and black pepper, to taste
- Lemon wedges, for serving
- Chopped fresh cilantro, for garnish

Instructions:

1. In a small bowl, combine the olive oil, minced garlic, ground cumin, ground coriander, ground paprika, ground cinnamon, ground ginger, ground turmeric, cayenne pepper, salt, and black pepper to make the Moroccan spice rub.
2. Place the chicken breasts in a shallow dish or a resealable plastic bag. Rub the Moroccan spice mixture evenly over the chicken breasts, ensuring they are well coated. Cover the dish or seal the bag, and refrigerate for at least 30 minutes to 1 hour to allow the flavors to meld.
3. Preheat your grill to medium-high heat.
4. Once the grill is hot, lightly oil the grates to prevent sticking.
5. Remove the chicken breasts from the marinade and discard any excess marinade.
6. Place the chicken breasts on the preheated grill. Grill for about 6-8 minutes per side, or until they are cooked through and have grill marks, flipping halfway through the cooking time.
7. While grilling, you can brush the chicken breasts with any remaining marinade for added flavor.

8. Once the chicken breasts are cooked through and reach an internal temperature of 165°F (75°C), remove them from the grill and transfer them to a serving platter.
9. Garnish the Moroccan spiced grilled chicken with chopped fresh cilantro and serve hot, accompanied by lemon wedges for squeezing over the chicken before eating.
10. Enjoy the aromatic and exotic flavors of this Moroccan-inspired grilled chicken dish!

Grilled Sausage and Peppers

Ingredients:

- 4 Italian sausages (sweet or spicy), about 1 pound
- 2 bell peppers (any color), sliced
- 1 large onion, sliced
- 2 tablespoons olive oil
- 2 cloves garlic, minced
- 1 teaspoon Italian seasoning
- Salt and black pepper, to taste
- Rolls, for serving

Instructions:

1. Preheat your grill to medium-high heat.
2. In a large bowl, toss the sliced bell peppers and onions with olive oil, minced garlic, Italian seasoning, salt, and black pepper until evenly coated.
3. Place the Italian sausages and the seasoned bell peppers and onions on the preheated grill.
4. Grill the sausages for about 12-15 minutes, turning occasionally, until they are cooked through and have grill marks on all sides.
5. Grill the bell peppers and onions for about 8-10 minutes, or until they are tender and slightly charred, stirring occasionally.
6. Once the sausages are cooked through and the bell peppers and onions are grilled to perfection, remove them from the grill and transfer them to a serving platter.
7. Optionally, grill the rolls for a minute or two until they are lightly toasted.
8. Serve the grilled sausages and peppers hot, either sliced and served in rolls or plated with a side of the grilled peppers and onions. Enjoy the hearty and flavorful combination of grilled sausages and vegetables!

Balsamic Glazed Grilled Pork Chops

Ingredients:

- 4 bone-in pork chops, about 1 inch thick
- Salt and black pepper, to taste
- 1/4 cup balsamic vinegar
- 2 tablespoons honey
- 2 cloves garlic, minced
- 1 teaspoon Dijon mustard
- 1 tablespoon olive oil
- Fresh rosemary sprigs, for garnish (optional)

Instructions:

1. Preheat your grill to medium-high heat.
2. Season the pork chops generously with salt and black pepper on both sides.
3. In a small saucepan, combine the balsamic vinegar, honey, minced garlic, and Dijon mustard. Bring the mixture to a simmer over medium heat, stirring occasionally, and cook for 5-7 minutes until it thickens slightly into a glaze. Remove from heat and set aside.
4. Brush the pork chops with olive oil on both sides to prevent sticking.
5. Place the pork chops on the preheated grill. Grill for about 4-5 minutes on each side, depending on thickness, until they are cooked through and reach an internal temperature of 145°F (63°C).
6. During the last few minutes of grilling, brush the pork chops with the balsamic glaze, reserving some for serving.
7. Once the pork chops are cooked and glazed, remove them from the grill and transfer them to a serving platter.
8. Drizzle the remaining balsamic glaze over the pork chops and garnish with fresh rosemary sprigs, if desired.
9. Serve the balsamic glazed grilled pork chops hot, accompanied by your favorite sides such as roasted vegetables, potatoes, or salad. Enjoy the delicious sweet and tangy flavors of this grilled pork dish!

Spicy Mango Grilled Chicken

Ingredients:

- 4 boneless, skinless chicken breasts
- 1 ripe mango, peeled and diced
- 2 tablespoons soy sauce
- 2 tablespoons honey
- 2 tablespoons lime juice
- 2 cloves garlic, minced
- 1 teaspoon grated fresh ginger
- 1 teaspoon chili powder
- 1/2 teaspoon ground cumin
- 1/4 teaspoon cayenne pepper (adjust to taste)
- Salt and black pepper, to taste
- Chopped fresh cilantro, for garnish
- Lime wedges, for serving

Instructions:

1. In a blender or food processor, combine the diced mango, soy sauce, honey, lime juice, minced garlic, grated ginger, chili powder, ground cumin, cayenne pepper, salt, and black pepper. Blend until smooth to make the marinade.
2. Place the chicken breasts in a shallow dish or a resealable plastic bag. Pour the mango marinade over the chicken, ensuring all pieces are well coated. Cover the dish or seal the bag, and refrigerate for at least 30 minutes to 1 hour to allow the flavors to meld.
3. Preheat your grill to medium-high heat.
4. Once the grill is hot, lightly oil the grates to prevent sticking.
5. Remove the chicken breasts from the marinade and discard any excess marinade.
6. Place the chicken breasts on the preheated grill. Grill for about 6-8 minutes per side, or until they are cooked through and have grill marks, flipping halfway through the cooking time.
7. While grilling, you can brush the chicken breasts with any remaining marinade for added flavor.
8. Once the chicken breasts are cooked through and reach an internal temperature of 165°F (75°C), remove them from the grill and transfer them to a serving platter.

9. Garnish the spicy mango grilled chicken with chopped fresh cilantro and serve hot, accompanied by lime wedges for squeezing over the chicken before eating.
10. Enjoy the sweet, spicy, and tangy flavors of this delicious grilled chicken dish!

Grilled Halloumi Cheese

Ingredients:

- 1 block halloumi cheese, sliced into 1/4-inch thick slices
- 1 tablespoon olive oil
- Freshly ground black pepper, to taste
- Fresh lemon wedges, for serving
- Optional: fresh herbs for garnish (such as mint or parsley)

Instructions:

1. Preheat your grill to medium-high heat.
2. Brush both sides of the halloumi slices with olive oil to prevent sticking.
3. Once the grill is hot, place the halloumi slices directly on the grill grates.
4. Grill the halloumi slices for about 2-3 minutes on each side, or until they develop grill marks and are golden brown.
5. Use a spatula to carefully flip the halloumi slices halfway through grilling.
6. Once the halloumi slices are grilled to perfection, remove them from the grill and transfer them to a serving platter.
7. Sprinkle freshly ground black pepper over the grilled halloumi slices.
8. Serve the grilled halloumi cheese hot, accompanied by fresh lemon wedges for squeezing over the cheese before eating.
9. Optionally, garnish the grilled halloumi with fresh herbs for added flavor and presentation.
10. Enjoy the deliciously salty and savory flavor of grilled halloumi cheese as a standalone appetizer or as part of a larger meal!

Honey Sriracha Grilled Wings

Ingredients:

- 2 pounds chicken wings, split into flats and drumettes
- Salt and black pepper, to taste
- 1/4 cup Sriracha sauce
- 1/4 cup honey
- 2 tablespoons soy sauce
- 2 tablespoons rice vinegar
- 2 cloves garlic, minced
- 1 tablespoon grated fresh ginger
- 1 tablespoon sesame oil
- Optional: sliced green onions and sesame seeds for garnish

Instructions:

1. Season the chicken wings with salt and black pepper to taste.
2. In a bowl, whisk together Sriracha sauce, honey, soy sauce, rice vinegar, minced garlic, grated ginger, and sesame oil to make the marinade.
3. Place the chicken wings in a large resealable plastic bag or shallow dish. Pour the marinade over the wings, ensuring they are well coated. Seal the bag or cover the dish, and marinate in the refrigerator for at least 1 hour, or overnight for best flavor.
4. Preheat your grill to medium-high heat.
5. Remove the chicken wings from the marinade, reserving the marinade for basting.
6. Lightly oil the grill grates to prevent sticking.
7. Place the chicken wings on the preheated grill. Grill for about 8-10 minutes per side, or until they are cooked through and have charred grill marks, turning occasionally.
8. During the last few minutes of grilling, brush the chicken wings with the reserved marinade for extra flavor.
9. Once the chicken wings are cooked through and glazed, remove them from the grill and transfer them to a serving platter.
10. Garnish the honey Sriracha grilled wings with sliced green onions and sesame seeds, if desired.

11. Serve the wings hot as a delicious appetizer or main dish, accompanied by your favorite dipping sauce. Enjoy the sweet, spicy, and savory flavors of these grilled wings!

Grilled Ratatouille

Ingredients:

- 1 eggplant, sliced into rounds
- 2 zucchinis, sliced into rounds
- 2 yellow squash, sliced into rounds
- 2 bell peppers (any color), sliced into strips
- 2 tomatoes, sliced into rounds
- 1 onion, sliced into rounds
- 3 cloves garlic, minced
- 1/4 cup olive oil
- Salt and black pepper, to taste
- 2 tablespoons balsamic vinegar
- Fresh basil leaves, for garnish

Instructions:

1. Preheat your grill to medium-high heat.
2. In a large bowl, toss the sliced eggplant, zucchini, yellow squash, bell peppers, tomatoes, onion, and minced garlic with olive oil until evenly coated. Season with salt and black pepper to taste.
3. Working in batches, grill the vegetables on the preheated grill until they are tender and have grill marks, about 3-4 minutes per side. Ensure to turn them halfway through grilling.
4. As the vegetables finish grilling, transfer them to a large serving platter or bowl.
5. Once all the vegetables are grilled, drizzle them with balsamic vinegar and gently toss to combine.
6. Garnish the grilled ratatouille with fresh basil leaves before serving.
7. Serve the grilled ratatouille warm or at room temperature as a delicious side dish or vegetarian main course. Enjoy the smoky flavors of grilled vegetables with the bright, tangy balsamic vinegar!

Argentinean Grilled Steak with Chimichurri Sauce

Ingredients:

For the Steak:

- 4 ribeye or sirloin steaks, about 1 inch thick
- Salt and black pepper, to taste
- Olive oil, for brushing

For the Chimichurri Sauce:

- 1 cup fresh parsley leaves, finely chopped
- 1/4 cup fresh cilantro leaves, finely chopped
- 4 cloves garlic, minced
- 2 tablespoons red wine vinegar
- 1/2 cup extra virgin olive oil
- 1 teaspoon dried oregano
- 1/2 teaspoon red pepper flakes (adjust to taste)
- Salt and black pepper, to taste
- Juice of 1/2 lemon (optional)

Instructions:

1. Preheat your grill to high heat.
2. Season the steaks generously with salt and black pepper on both sides.
3. Brush the steaks with olive oil to prevent sticking.
4. Place the steaks on the preheated grill and cook for about 4-5 minutes on each side for medium-rare, or adjust cooking time to your desired level of doneness.
5. While the steaks are grilling, prepare the chimichurri sauce. In a bowl, combine the finely chopped parsley, cilantro, minced garlic, red wine vinegar, extra virgin olive oil, dried oregano, red pepper flakes, salt, and black pepper. Stir well to combine.
6. Once the steaks are cooked to your liking, remove them from the grill and let them rest for a few minutes.
7. Slice the steaks against the grain into thin slices.

8. Serve the grilled steak slices hot, accompanied by chimichurri sauce drizzled over the top or served on the side.
9. Optionally, squeeze some fresh lemon juice over the steak slices for added brightness.
10. Enjoy the juicy and flavorful Argentinean grilled steak with the vibrant and herby chimichurri sauce!

Cajun Grilled Cornbread

Ingredients:

- 1 cup yellow cornmeal
- 1 cup all-purpose flour
- 1 tablespoon baking powder
- 1/2 teaspoon baking soda
- 1/2 teaspoon salt
- 2 tablespoons granulated sugar
- 1/4 cup unsalted butter, melted
- 1 cup buttermilk
- 2 large eggs
- 1 tablespoon Cajun seasoning
- 1/2 cup shredded cheddar cheese (optional)
- 1 jalapeño, seeded and finely diced (optional)

Instructions:

1. Preheat your grill to medium heat.
2. In a large mixing bowl, combine the cornmeal, flour, baking powder, baking soda, salt, and granulated sugar. Mix well to combine.
3. In a separate bowl, whisk together the melted butter, buttermilk, and eggs until well combined.
4. Pour the wet ingredients into the dry ingredients and stir until just combined. Be careful not to overmix.
5. Stir in the Cajun seasoning until evenly distributed throughout the batter.
6. Optionally, fold in the shredded cheddar cheese and diced jalapeño for added flavor and heat.
7. Pour the batter into a greased 9x9-inch square baking dish or a cast-iron skillet.
8. Place the baking dish or skillet on the preheated grill and close the lid.
9. Grill the cornbread for about 20-25 minutes, or until a toothpick inserted into the center comes out clean and the top is golden brown.
10. Once the cornbread is cooked through, remove it from the grill and let it cool slightly before slicing.

11. Serve the Cajun grilled cornbread warm, either as a side dish to complement your favorite barbecue or as a standalone snack. Enjoy the smoky flavor and Cajun spice-infused cornbread straight from the grill!

Grilled Stuffed Zucchini

Ingredients:

- 4 medium zucchinis
- 1 tablespoon olive oil
- Salt and black pepper, to taste
- 1/2 cup cooked quinoa or rice
- 1/2 cup cherry tomatoes, halved
- 1/2 cup crumbled feta cheese
- 1/4 cup chopped fresh basil leaves
- 2 cloves garlic, minced
- 1/4 teaspoon red pepper flakes (optional)
- Grated Parmesan cheese, for topping (optional)

Instructions:

1. Preheat your grill to medium heat.
2. Cut the zucchinis in half lengthwise. Using a spoon, scoop out the flesh from the center of each zucchini half, leaving about a 1/4-inch border around the edges. Reserve the scooped-out flesh.
3. Brush the zucchini halves with olive oil and season with salt and black pepper.
4. In a mixing bowl, combine the cooked quinoa or rice, cherry tomatoes, crumbled feta cheese, chopped fresh basil leaves, minced garlic, and red pepper flakes (if using). Mix well to combine.
5. Spoon the quinoa or rice mixture into the hollowed-out center of each zucchini half, pressing down gently to pack the filling.
6. Place the stuffed zucchini halves on the preheated grill, filling-side up. Close the grill lid and cook for about 10-15 minutes, or until the zucchini is tender and the filling is heated through.
7. Optionally, sprinkle grated Parmesan cheese over the stuffed zucchini during the last few minutes of grilling.
8. Once the stuffed zucchini is cooked through and the cheese is melted and bubbly, remove them from the grill.
9. Serve the grilled stuffed zucchini hot as a delicious and nutritious side dish or vegetarian main course. Enjoy the flavorful combination of tender zucchini filled with savory quinoa or rice, tomatoes, and feta cheese!

Lemon Garlic Grilled Shrimp

Ingredients:

- 1 pound large shrimp, peeled and deveined
- 2 tablespoons olive oil
- 3 cloves garlic, minced
- Zest of 1 lemon
- Juice of 1 lemon
- 1 tablespoon chopped fresh parsley
- Salt and black pepper, to taste
- Lemon wedges, for serving
- Skewers, soaked in water for 30 minutes (if using wooden skewers)

Instructions:

1. In a bowl, combine the olive oil, minced garlic, lemon zest, lemon juice, chopped fresh parsley, salt, and black pepper. Mix well to make the marinade.
2. Add the peeled and deveined shrimp to the marinade and toss to coat evenly. Allow the shrimp to marinate for about 15-30 minutes in the refrigerator.
3. Preheat your grill to medium-high heat.
4. Thread the marinated shrimp onto skewers, dividing them evenly among the skewers.
5. Once the grill is hot, lightly oil the grates to prevent sticking.
6. Place the shrimp skewers on the preheated grill. Grill for about 2-3 minutes per side, or until the shrimp are pink and opaque, and have grill marks.
7. While grilling, you can brush the shrimp with any remaining marinade for added flavor.
8. Once the shrimp are cooked through, remove them from the grill and transfer them to a serving platter.
9. Serve the lemon garlic grilled shrimp hot, accompanied by lemon wedges for squeezing over the shrimp before eating.
10. Enjoy the bright and zesty flavors of these delicious grilled shrimp as a flavorful appetizer or main dish!

BBQ Pulled Pork Sandwiches

Ingredients:

- 2 pounds pork shoulder (also known as pork butt), trimmed of excess fat
- Salt and black pepper, to taste
- 1 tablespoon olive oil
- 1 onion, finely chopped
- 3 cloves garlic, minced
- 1 cup barbecue sauce, plus extra for serving
- 1 cup chicken or vegetable broth
- Hamburger buns or sandwich rolls, for serving
- Coleslaw, for topping (optional)

Instructions:

1. Season the pork shoulder with salt and black pepper on all sides.
2. In a large skillet or Dutch oven, heat the olive oil over medium-high heat. Add the pork shoulder and sear on all sides until browned, about 3-4 minutes per side. Remove the pork shoulder from the skillet and set aside.
3. In the same skillet, add the chopped onion and garlic. Cook, stirring occasionally, until the onion is softened and translucent, about 3-4 minutes.
4. Return the seared pork shoulder to the skillet with the onion and garlic.
5. Pour the barbecue sauce and chicken or vegetable broth over the pork shoulder, ensuring it is well coated.
6. Cover the skillet with a lid or aluminum foil and reduce the heat to low. Simmer the pork shoulder for about 6-8 hours, or until it is very tender and easily shreds with a fork. You can also cook it in a slow cooker on low for 8 hours.
7. Once the pork shoulder is cooked through and tender, remove it from the skillet or slow cooker and transfer it to a cutting board. Use two forks to shred the meat.
8. Return the shredded pork to the skillet or slow cooker and toss it in the sauce until evenly coated.
9. To serve, spoon the BBQ pulled pork onto hamburger buns or sandwich rolls. Top with extra barbecue sauce and coleslaw, if desired.
10. Serve the BBQ pulled pork sandwiches hot, accompanied by your favorite sides such as potato chips, pickles, or a side salad. Enjoy the delicious and tender pulled pork with its sweet and tangy barbecue flavor!

Grilled Pineapple Slices

Ingredients:

- 1 fresh pineapple
- Olive oil or melted butter, for brushing (optional)
- Honey or brown sugar, for drizzling (optional)
- Cinnamon, for sprinkling (optional)
- Vanilla ice cream, for serving (optional)

Instructions:

1. Preheat your grill to medium-high heat.
2. Slice off the top and bottom of the pineapple, then stand it upright on one end. Using a sharp knife, carefully slice off the skin, working your way around the pineapple from top to bottom, removing all the outer skin and "eyes."
3. Lay the peeled pineapple on its side and slice it into rounds, about 1/2 to 1 inch thick.
4. Optionally, brush both sides of the pineapple slices lightly with olive oil or melted butter to prevent sticking and enhance flavor.
5. Place the pineapple slices directly on the preheated grill grates.
6. Grill the pineapple slices for about 2-3 minutes on each side, or until they develop grill marks and are caramelized.
7. Optionally, while grilling, you can drizzle honey or sprinkle brown sugar and cinnamon over the pineapple slices for added sweetness and flavor.
8. Once the pineapple slices are grilled to your liking, remove them from the grill and transfer them to a serving platter.
9. Serve the grilled pineapple slices hot as a delicious and refreshing dessert or snack.
10. Optionally, serve the grilled pineapple slices with a scoop of vanilla ice cream for a delightful combination of sweet and tangy flavors and hot and cold temperatures.
11. Enjoy the smoky and caramelized flavor of grilled pineapple straight from the grill!

Buffalo Grilled Cauliflower

Ingredients:

- 1 head cauliflower, cut into florets
- 2 tablespoons olive oil
- Salt and black pepper, to taste
- 1/2 cup buffalo sauce
- 2 tablespoons melted butter (or olive oil for a dairy-free option)
- 1 tablespoon honey (optional, for sweetness)
- Ranch or blue cheese dressing, for serving (optional)
- Chopped fresh parsley or cilantro, for garnish (optional)
- Celery sticks, for serving (optional)

Instructions:

1. Preheat your grill to medium-high heat.
2. In a large bowl, toss the cauliflower florets with olive oil until evenly coated. Season with salt and black pepper to taste.
3. Place the cauliflower florets on the preheated grill. Grill for about 8-10 minutes, turning occasionally, until they are tender and have grill marks.
4. In a separate bowl, whisk together the buffalo sauce, melted butter (or olive oil), and honey (if using) until well combined.
5. Remove the grilled cauliflower from the grill and transfer them to a clean bowl.
6. Pour the buffalo sauce mixture over the grilled cauliflower and toss until the cauliflower is evenly coated.
7. Return the cauliflower to the grill and cook for an additional 2-3 minutes, allowing the sauce to caramelize slightly.
8. Once the buffalo grilled cauliflower is cooked through and glazed, remove it from the grill and transfer it to a serving platter.
9. Garnish the buffalo grilled cauliflower with chopped fresh parsley or cilantro, if desired.
10. Serve hot with ranch or blue cheese dressing on the side for dipping, and celery sticks for added crunch. Enjoy the spicy and flavorful buffalo grilled cauliflower as a delicious appetizer or side dish!

Mediterranean Grilled Chicken Wraps

Ingredients:

- 4 boneless, skinless chicken breasts
- 2 tablespoons olive oil
- 2 cloves garlic, minced
- 1 teaspoon dried oregano
- 1 teaspoon dried thyme
- 1 teaspoon paprika
- 1/2 teaspoon ground cumin
- Salt and black pepper, to taste
- 4 large whole wheat or spinach tortillas
- 1 cup hummus
- 1 cup diced tomatoes
- 1 cup diced cucumbers
- 1/2 cup crumbled feta cheese
- 1/4 cup sliced black olives
- Fresh parsley, chopped, for garnish
- Lemon wedges, for serving

Instructions:

1. In a bowl, combine the olive oil, minced garlic, dried oregano, dried thyme, paprika, ground cumin, salt, and black pepper to make the marinade.
2. Place the chicken breasts in a shallow dish or a resealable plastic bag. Pour the marinade over the chicken, ensuring all pieces are well coated. Cover the dish or seal the bag, and refrigerate for at least 30 minutes to 1 hour to allow the flavors to meld.
3. Preheat your grill to medium-high heat.
4. Once the grill is hot, remove the chicken breasts from the marinade and discard any excess marinade.
5. Grill the chicken breasts for about 6-8 minutes per side, or until they are cooked through and have grill marks, flipping halfway through the cooking time.
6. While the chicken is grilling, warm the tortillas on the grill for about 1-2 minutes on each side, until they are lightly toasted and pliable.
7. Once the chicken breasts are cooked through, remove them from the grill and let them rest for a few minutes before slicing them into strips.

8. To assemble the wraps, spread a layer of hummus over each warmed tortilla.
9. Arrange the sliced grilled chicken, diced tomatoes, diced cucumbers, crumbled feta cheese, and sliced black olives down the center of each tortilla.
10. Sprinkle chopped fresh parsley over the fillings.
11. Fold in the sides of each tortilla and then roll them up tightly into wraps.
12. Serve the Mediterranean grilled chicken wraps immediately, accompanied by lemon wedges for squeezing over the wraps before eating.
13. Enjoy these flavorful and satisfying wraps as a delicious lunch or dinner option!

Grilled Asparagus with Parmesan

Ingredients:

- 1 pound fresh asparagus spears, woody ends trimmed
- 2 tablespoons olive oil
- Salt and black pepper, to taste
- 1/4 cup grated Parmesan cheese
- Lemon wedges, for serving (optional)

Instructions:

1. Preheat your grill to medium-high heat.
2. In a large bowl, toss the asparagus spears with olive oil until evenly coated.
3. Season the asparagus with salt and black pepper to taste.
4. Place the asparagus spears directly on the preheated grill grates.
5. Grill the asparagus for about 5-7 minutes, turning occasionally, until they are tender and have grill marks.
6. Once the asparagus is grilled to your liking, remove them from the grill and transfer them to a serving platter.
7. Sprinkle the grated Parmesan cheese over the grilled asparagus while they are still warm, allowing the cheese to melt slightly.
8. Optionally, serve the grilled asparagus with lemon wedges for squeezing over the top before eating.
9. Enjoy the delicious and flavorful grilled asparagus with Parmesan as a tasty side dish to complement any meal!

Tequila Lime Grilled Chicken

Ingredients:

- 4 boneless, skinless chicken breasts
- 1/4 cup tequila
- Zest and juice of 2 limes
- 2 tablespoons olive oil
- 2 cloves garlic, minced
- 1 teaspoon chili powder
- 1 teaspoon ground cumin
- 1/2 teaspoon paprika
- Salt and black pepper, to taste
- Fresh cilantro, chopped, for garnish (optional)
- Lime wedges, for serving

Instructions:

1. In a bowl, combine the tequila, lime zest, lime juice, olive oil, minced garlic, chili powder, ground cumin, paprika, salt, and black pepper. Mix well to make the marinade.
2. Place the chicken breasts in a shallow dish or a resealable plastic bag. Pour the marinade over the chicken, ensuring all pieces are well coated. Cover the dish or seal the bag, and refrigerate for at least 30 minutes to 1 hour to allow the flavors to meld.
3. Preheat your grill to medium-high heat.
4. Once the grill is hot, remove the chicken breasts from the marinade and discard any excess marinade.
5. Place the chicken breasts on the preheated grill. Grill for about 6-8 minutes per side, or until they are cooked through and have grill marks, flipping halfway through the cooking time.
6. While grilling, you can brush the chicken breasts with any remaining marinade for added flavor.
7. Once the chicken breasts are cooked through and reach an internal temperature of 165°F (75°C), remove them from the grill and transfer them to a serving platter.
8. Garnish the tequila lime grilled chicken with chopped fresh cilantro, if desired, and serve hot with lime wedges for squeezing over the chicken before eating.

9. Enjoy the bright and zesty flavors of this delicious tequila lime grilled chicken!

Grilled Sweet Potato Wedges

Ingredients:

- 2 large sweet potatoes
- 2 tablespoons olive oil
- 1 teaspoon smoked paprika
- 1 teaspoon garlic powder
- 1/2 teaspoon ground cumin
- 1/2 teaspoon chili powder
- Salt and black pepper, to taste
- Fresh parsley or cilantro, chopped, for garnish (optional)
- Lime wedges, for serving (optional)

Instructions:

1. Preheat your grill to medium-high heat.
2. Scrub the sweet potatoes clean and pat them dry with paper towels.
3. Slice each sweet potato lengthwise into wedges, about 1/2 to 3/4 inch thick.
4. In a large bowl, toss the sweet potato wedges with olive oil until evenly coated.
5. In a small bowl, mix together the smoked paprika, garlic powder, ground cumin, chili powder, salt, and black pepper.
6. Sprinkle the spice mixture over the sweet potato wedges and toss until they are evenly coated with the spices.
7. Once the grill is hot, place the sweet potato wedges directly on the preheated grill grates.
8. Grill the sweet potato wedges for about 8-10 minutes per side, or until they are tender and have grill marks, flipping halfway through the cooking time.
9. Once the sweet potato wedges are grilled to your liking, remove them from the grill and transfer them to a serving platter.
10. Optionally, garnish the grilled sweet potato wedges with chopped fresh parsley or cilantro for added flavor and freshness.
11. Serve the grilled sweet potato wedges hot, accompanied by lime wedges for squeezing over the wedges before eating, if desired.
12. Enjoy these smoky and flavorful grilled sweet potato wedges as a delicious side dish or snack!

Ginger Soy Grilled Tofu

Ingredients:

- 1 block (14-16 oz) extra firm tofu, pressed and drained
- 3 tablespoons soy sauce
- 2 tablespoons rice vinegar
- 1 tablespoon sesame oil
- 1 tablespoon honey or maple syrup
- 2 cloves garlic, minced
- 1 tablespoon fresh ginger, grated
- 1 tablespoon olive oil (for grilling)
- Sesame seeds, for garnish
- Green onions, chopped, for garnish

Instructions:

1. Press the tofu to remove excess water. Place the tofu block between two plates and weigh the top plate down with cans or something heavy. Let it press for about 20-30 minutes, then drain off any released liquid.
2. In a shallow dish or a resealable plastic bag, whisk together the soy sauce, rice vinegar, sesame oil, honey or maple syrup, minced garlic, and grated ginger to make the marinade.
3. Slice the pressed tofu block into 1/2-inch thick slices, then place them in the marinade. Ensure all slices are well-coated. Marinate for at least 30 minutes, or up to overnight in the refrigerator.
4. Preheat your grill to medium-high heat. Brush the grill grates with olive oil to prevent sticking.
5. Remove the tofu slices from the marinade and shake off any excess. Reserve the marinade for basting.
6. Place the tofu slices directly on the preheated grill. Grill for about 3-4 minutes on each side, or until grill marks form and the tofu is heated through.
7. While grilling, baste the tofu slices with the reserved marinade for extra flavor.
8. Once the tofu is grilled to your desired level of crispiness, remove from the grill and transfer to a serving plate.
9. Sprinkle sesame seeds and chopped green onions over the grilled tofu for garnish.

10. Serve hot as a delicious vegetarian main dish or protein addition to salads, stir-fries, or grain bowls.
11. Enjoy the flavorful and tender ginger soy grilled tofu!

BBQ Jackfruit Sandwiches

Ingredients:

- 2 cans young green jackfruit in brine or water
- 1 tablespoon olive oil
- 1 onion, diced
- 2 cloves garlic, minced
- 1 cup barbecue sauce
- 1/2 cup vegetable broth or water
- Salt and black pepper, to taste
- Hamburger buns or sandwich rolls, for serving
- Coleslaw, for topping (optional)

Instructions:

1. Drain and rinse the canned jackfruit. Use your fingers to pull apart the jackfruit pieces, separating the fibrous parts.
2. In a skillet, heat olive oil over medium heat. Add diced onion and minced garlic, sautéing until softened and fragrant.
3. Add the pulled jackfruit to the skillet and cook for a few minutes until it starts to brown slightly.
4. Pour in the barbecue sauce and vegetable broth (or water) and stir to combine. Bring the mixture to a simmer.
5. Reduce the heat to low and let the jackfruit simmer for about 15-20 minutes, stirring occasionally, until it's tender and has absorbed the flavors of the sauce.
6. Taste and adjust the seasoning with salt and black pepper if needed.
7. Once the jackfruit is cooked through and tender, remove it from the heat.
8. To assemble the sandwiches, spoon the BBQ jackfruit onto hamburger buns or sandwich rolls.
9. Optionally, top with coleslaw for added crunch and freshness.
10. Serve the BBQ jackfruit sandwiches hot and enjoy the delicious meaty texture and smoky flavor of this vegetarian alternative to pulled pork!

www.ingramcontent.com/pod-product-compliance
Lightning Source LLC
LaVergne TN
LVHW081618060526
838201LV00054B/2298